Choosing to Be Grateful

Cycle A Gospel Sermons for Pentecost 23 Through Thanksgiving Day

Albert G. Butzer, III

CSS Publishing Company, Inc.
Lima, Ohio

CHOOSING TO BE GRATEFUL
CYCLE A GOSPEL SERMONS FOR
PENTECOST 23 THROUGH THANKSGIVING

FIRST EDITION
Copyright © 2016
by CSS Publishing Co., Inc.

Published by CSS Publishing Company, Inc., Lima, Ohio 45807. All rights reserved. No part of this publication may be reproduced in any manner whatsoever without the prior permission of the publisher, except in the case of brief quotations embodied in critical articles and reviews. Inquiries should be addressed to: CSS Publishing Company, Inc., Permissions Department, 5450 N. Dixie Highway, Lima, Ohio 45807.

Library of Congress Cataloging-in-Publication Data

Names: Butzer, Albert G., 1954- author.
Title: Choosing to be grateful : gospel sermons for Pentecost (last third) Cycle A / Albert G. Butzer, III.
Description: FIRST EDITION. | Lima : CSS Publishing Company, 2016.
Identifiers: LCCN 2016024784 | ISBN 9780788028694
Subjects: LCSH: Bible. Gospels--Sermons. | Sermons, American--21st century. |
  Pentecost season--Sermons. | Church year sermons. | Common lectionary (1992). Year A.
Classification: LCC BS2555.54 .B88 2016 | DDC 252/.64--dc23
LC record available at https://lccn.loc.gov/2016024784

For more information about CSS Publishing Company resources, visit our website at www.csspub.com, email us at csr@csspub.com, or call (800) 241-4056.

e-book:
ISBN-13: 978-0-7880-28XX-X
ISBN-10: 0-7880-28XX-X

ISBN-13: 978-0-7880-2869-4
ISBN-10: 0-7880-2869-3

PRINTED IN USA

To Betsy...

... who has taught me most everything I know about joy, beauty, grace, hospitality, and love.

Preface

At its best, preaching is incarnational ministry. The Word becomes Flesh through the exhale of the preacher and the inhale of the listener. The dusty word becomes the Living Word as it gets up off the page and wanders into the heartbeat of everyday life. Those who are in Christ experience the Christ within — and new creation has begun.

Preaching is not entertainment or lecturing or Bible study. It is not debate or instruction or reprimand. Preaching is intimate communication between God and God's people — what Barbara Brown Taylor calls "an ancient courtship." And the preacher is the "go-between, the courier" never entering the sermon without the congregation — so that the sermon begins and ends with them. As such, preaching is risky business. And good preachers quake every time they step into the preaching moment.

Al Butzer understands this privilege, this power, this promise of preaching, He has been at it a long time, and his quaking is as fresh today as it was 35 years ago. His sermons crawl inside our lives, because his life is much like ours. He does not pontificate; he persuades. He does not prescribe; he wonders. He does not scold; he inspires. Through story and metaphor and creative twists of theology, he widens the lens of our lives and helps us see in new ways.

Imagine yourself on a sailboat for four days in a wet, raging wind — a vacation gone terribly awry. And yet Al shares his learning from that experience — a lesson of gratitude. Imagine arguing with Jesus about serving Caesar or serving God. We learn that it is a matter of prioritizing — not compartmentalizing. Imagine seeing yourself as a convicted hypocrite, as we all are — and receiving the freedom of unconditional forgiveness. Imagine God as an angry old man — transformed by this preacher into a gentle and generous host. Al Butzer helps us see and feel and embrace grace — amidst the ugly, beautiful truth of our living.

For fifteen years, it was my privilege to be in a pastor's spiritual direction group with Al. Eight of us met monthly for three hours — and we invited each other to share our individual spiritual journeys — with all the personal and professional twists along the way. With humor, curiosity, and deep pastoral skill, Al would often dig deep into the God in our lives and open up fresh vistas of grace and truth. This same wisdom and gentle pushing is woven throughout the sermons in this book. We are comforted and afflicted at the same time, and we leave the sermon as changed people.

Al is a theologian as well as a preacher — deeply rooted in the soil of creative Christian thinkers (Douglas John Hall, Tom Long, John Calvin, Marcus Borg, Barbara Brown Taylor, Martin Marty, Craig Barnes). But this thoughtful theology becomes a flesh and blood experience, so that we can taste and smell and feel the Word. And as a committed parish pastor, Al conveys his deep love for the church, even in the shadows of our current diminished state.

Al is a writer as well as a preacher. So he preaches the old-fashioned way. His manuscripts are polished and offered as a treasure of language and image. No screens or video clips or wandering around the sanctuary are necessary. Like a vintage wine, the Word of God has fermented inside the heart and mind of this preacher until its rich nectar has settled into mature gospel. Such a careful crafting of the sermon assures that the preached word focuses on God and not the preacher. And when the preacher shines through, it is as a forgiven sinner and a transformed disciple.

This collection of sermons can serve as a devotional guide, a small group resource, a stimulus for curious preachers to find their own voice. It is emotionally intelligent, biblically sound, and spiritually nourishing. In these pages you will find a living Christ who makes all things new. Enjoy!

Susan Andrews
Pastor, Preacher, Writer
Moderator of the 215th General Assembly of the Presbyterian Church, USA

Table of Contents

Introduction   9

Proper 23 / Pentecost 19 / Ordinary Time 28
    All Are Invited, but...   11
    Matthew 22:1-14

Proper 24 / Pentecost 20 / Ordinary Time 29
    Stamped with God's Own Image   17
    Matthew 22:15-22

Proper 25 / Pentecost 21 / Ordinary Time 30
    The Rule of Love   23
    Matthew 22:34-46

Reformation Sunday
    The Word Above All Earthly Powers   29
    John 8:31-36

All Saints Day
    Blessed to Be Among the Company of Mourners   35
    Matthew 5:1-12

Proper 26 / Pentecost 22 / Ordinary Time 31
    Practicing What We Preach   41
    Matthew 23:1-12

Proper 27 / Pentecost 23 / Ordinary Time 32
    Are You Ready to Wait?   47
    Matthew 25:1-13

Proper 28 / Pentecost 24 / Ordinary Time 33
    The Gospel We Preach   53
    Matthew 25:14-30

Christ the King (Proper 29) /
    Pentecost 25 / Ordinary Time 34
  The Judge of the Living and the Dead   59
  Matthew 25:31-46

Thanksgiving Day
  Choosing to Be Grateful   65
  Luke 17:11-19

Introduction

Some people express their beliefs by saying, "I believe in God the Father almighty, maker of heaven and earth, and in Jesus Christ, his only Son our Lord." While I too affirm all of that, my faith began not with a creed, but with the church and its people.

- It was the church that taught me about God, Jesus, and the Holy Spirit.
- It was the church that taught me to worship and pray and serve.
- It was the church that taught me to love the Bible and regard it as a constant companion and trustworthy friend.
- It was the church, through the voice of its ministers, Sunday school teachers, youth leaders, and members that called me to preach the word and administer the sacraments.

I love the weekly opportunity the people of my congregation give me to try to help them make sense of the intersection of life and faith. As Christians we live our lives with one leg in the ancient sacred world of the Bible and the other leg in our modern scientific world. The job of the preacher is to try to make some sort of holy sense of the intersection of these two worlds. At least, that is what my professors and mentors taught me. It is a great honor and a sacred responsibility to struggle to do this, as well as a weekly dose of humility. Sometimes the preaching task goes well and sometimes not so well, as careful readers of this book will quickly discern!

Among my favorite quotes is something attributed to Ernest Hemingway. Hemingway once said, "Most of the time I write as well as I can; occasionally I write even better." When applied to the task of preaching, these words remind us that faithful preaching is a lot of disciplined work, with occasional moments of inspiration that come from some source outside of ourselves. Blessed is the preacher who knows the true source of a sermon's inspiration and responds to it with deep gratitude!

The preaching task must never be separated from congregational life, and congregational life must never be separated from public life. I love the church in all of its wonderful complexity and see the church's theological diversity as one of her strengths rather than a weakness. Unfortunately, most of the time the media rarely catches on to this diversity, instead allowing certain intolerant loudmouths to speak for the Christian faith as a whole. We in the mainline Protestant tradition have a great opportunity to speak a different word: not words of anger and judgment but words of grace; not words of hate but words of love; not words that close people out, but words that include and welcome.

I do worry about the future of the church in America. Many people who once supported churches with their prayers and presence no longer do so. The rapid rise of those whom the Pew Research Center calls, "Nones" (those who state their religious preference as *none*) makes it hard for me to imagine how the church will reach out and draw them back.

Fortunately, the future of the church does not depend upon me or upon you. It depends on Christ. Just as he once calmed the wind and the waves and kept that tiny boat (the church!) from sinking, so he still has his hand on the tiller and is steering his church confidently through the turbulent and chaotic waves of our time into a future which belongs to him. As long as he is doing so, there will always be a sacred task for those who are called to preach.

— Albert G. Butzer, III

Proper 23 / Pentecost 19 / Ordinary Time 28
Matthew 22:1-14

All Are Invited, but ...

Go therefore into the main streets, and invite everyone you find to the wedding banquet.
— Matthew 22:9

When you arrive at the church to attend a wedding, most often someone will hand you a program or a bulletin, which contains not only the order of the service but also the names of the wedding participants. It's a helpful thing to have in hand, especially if you struggle to remember people's names. Maybe you ask yourself: "What are the first names of the groom's parents?" "Is that young woman the maid or matron of honor?" Perhaps you think, "I know that I met that groomsman recently. I just can't remember his name." In the world of sports, we sometimes say, "You can't tell the players without a program." Similarly a wedding program can be a huge help. Now if only we could persuade the participants to wear numbers on the backs of their dresses and tuxedos!

Something like a wedding program would help us understand today's scripture from Matthew. Jesus' story is a parable that defies easy explanation. In fact, it is what scholars call "an allegorical parable," which means that things in the story actually stand for other things. It's hard enough to make sense of the plain meaning of the story; it's even more so when everything in the story stands for something else. Here's one way to think about it:

The king in the story	=	God
The son	=	Jesus
The marriage feast	=	the relationship into which God calls and invites us

The slaves	=	the prophets of Israel
Those invited	=	those who first rejected Jesus

The story unfolds like this: the king planned a great wedding celebration for his son, Jesus. Long before the day of the wedding the king sent out "save the date" postcards, so that everybody would reserve the date. Then came the formal invitations, each of them addressed in beautifully, hand-written calligraphy. On the day of the wedding, the king sent out his servants saying, "The day is here. Come to the celebration." But those who had been invited chose *not* to come. The king sent more servants saying, "Look, the dinner is ready, the fatted calves have been prepared, the wine has been poured. Won't you please come to the celebration?"

"But," says the gospel writer, "they made light of the invitation," and went back to their farms and jobs as if this were any other ordinary day. Indeed, adds Matthew, the refusal of the guests even turned violent and led to the death of some and the destruction of their city, which Bible scholars feel is Matthew's way of referring to the destruction of Jerusalem in 70 AD at the hands of the Romans.[1]

What was the king to do? He had a son who was eager to marry and a wedding reception where the salad was wilting and the meat was growing cold. He had to come up with a different strategy. "Go into the main streets," said the king, "and invite everyone you find to the wedding banquet." The slaves did as they were told and they brought back all whom they found, both good and bad, so that the wedding hall was filled with guests."

Undoubtedly, the first-century Christians could relate to this story because it *mirrored* their own story. It was playing out in their very midst. As the gospel message spread from its mostly Jewish beginnings and reached out into the main streets of towns and cities, welcoming Jews as well as Gentiles, the good as well as the bad, the very nature of their community, the very fabric of their church family, began to change.

This gospel story is still playing out in our day and age. Most everybody knows that the institutional church here in America is in trouble. Some people claim that 90% of all American churches are either on a plateau or losing members. Today, according to the Pew Research Center the fastest growing religious sub group in America is made up of people called "nones," that's N-O-N-E-S. When asked to state their religious preference, they simply reply: none.[2] These people once filled our pews but now have drifted away to become nones, leaving us asking whom, if anyone, will sit down at the marriage feast and eat from the messianic banquet table. Just as the king once sent his servants into the streets of the city to invite in those they met, both good and bad, so now the king sends us to do the inviting so that the wedding hall — the church — might be filled with guests.

This is a scary idea to say the least! It's one thing to invite your friends and neighbors, people who are just like you. It's something much more threatening to invite in *everyone*, the good and the bad, so that the wedding hall will be filled. It raises all sorts of troubling questions: What if they don't look like us? What if they speak with accents? What if they come from another part of town? What if they are different?

On top of all that, we also have one more thing to worry about... what if we do find the courage to invite them, only to learn that the king finds their presence problematic? Are you as perplexed by the parable as I when the king starts acting like a nightclub bouncer and says to one of the guests, "How did you get in here without the proper clothes? This is a wedding banquet, after all. The least you can do is show up wearing the right kind of clothes!"

With every ounce of decency we possess, we want to protest such treatment. We want to say to the king, "You just asked us to go into the streets and invite in *everyone*, the good and the bad. How can you hold it against them if they don't have the right kind of clothes? Doesn't this seem to contradict the open, gracious invitation you just asked us to extend?"

Here is another place in the parable at which we need that wedding program to help us know who's who and what's what. Remember in an allegorical parable, everything stands for something else. This means that the guest who showed up without a wedding garment may stand for all those Christians who have found their way into the church, but have failed to clothe themselves in the garments of Christ, symbols of the new life he invites us to put on.

And what are those garments? Perhaps the members of Matthew's church would have been familiar with the garments spelled out in Paul's Letter to the Colossians. "Clothe yourselves with compassion," wrote Paul, "and kindness, humility, meekness, and patience.... Above all, clothe yourselves with love, which binds everything together in perfect harmony" (Colossians 3:12-14).

Some of you may recall the time when certain restaurants had a dress code, where they expected men, for example, to wear a sport coat. If you showed up at the restaurant and were clearly underdressed, the management would not refuse to let you in. Instead, they would discreetly loan you a sport coat so that you could fit in.

There is a part of me that wishes that the king in the gospel story had used a similar discretion. Rather than chastising the guest for being underdressed, rather than tossing him out on his ear, tossing him, in fact, into outer darkness, I wish that the king had been a bit more gracious and generous. I wish that the king had said, "Sir, you can't attend the party dressed like that. But, look, here is a spare wedding garment. I would be pleased to loan it to you."

But no, the king in the parable gets angry, not because a single guest was underdressed. Remember, he stands for something else. Rather, the king gets angry because many who called themselves Christians were not acting the way

Christians are supposed to act. They failed to clothe themselves in those Christ-like garments of compassion, kindness, meekness, patience, and above all else — love. As a result, the king's wrath burned hot against them and he threw them out because they failed to live up to their end of the bargain.

It's true that all are invited, the good as well as the bad, but it's also true that there is a certain code of conduct for those who accept the invitation and want to call themselves "Christian." As Jesus stated earlier in Matthew's gospel, "Not everyone who says to me, 'Lord, Lord,' will enter the kingdom of heaven, but only the one who does the will of my Father in heaven" (Matthew 7:21). In other words, you can't just talk the talk. You also have to walk the walk.

In light of all of this, here's what I am going to do. Tonight before I go to bed, I'm going to write out a list of the Christlike garments that Paul mentions in Colossians — compassion, kindness, meekness, patience, and above all else love. I'll put it in a visible place in my closet. Then tomorrow morning when I open the closet door and say to myself, "What shall I wear today?" I will come face-to-face with this little list and then try, if only for that day, to wear one or more of these virtues, I mean really let it show. I'll try to do the same the next day and the day after that. By doing so, other people might even notice that I am really trying to wear the garments of faith, really trying to live the life Christ calls me to live. And who knows, but the king might even find a seat for me and ask me to stay at that wedding feast in the messianic banquet hall.

Amen.

---

1. Ronald J. Allen and Clark M. Williamson, *Preaching the Gospel Without Blaming the Jews* (Louisville: Westminster John Knox Press, 2004), p. 77.
2. Pew Research: *Religion and Public Life*, October 9, 2002.

Proper 24 / Pentecost 20 / Ordinary Time 29
Matthew 22:15-22

Stamped with God's Own Image

And they brought him a denarius. Then he said to them, "Whose head is this and whose title?"
— Matthew 22:19

Recent DNA tests reveal that a software engineer from South Carolina shared an exact match to the maternal mitochondrial DNA of King Richard III of England. As you may know, the King's bones were discovered in 2012 under a parking lot in England on land that was once a friary. The bones showed signs of a spinal deformity the king was known to have had. The skull showed wounds consistent with accounts of his death in 1485 at the Battle of Bosworth Field. In March 2015, some 530 years after his death on the battlefield, and after three years of DNA testing, the King finally received a proper royal burial in an Anglican Cathedral church.

Thanks to the precision of DNA testing, David Brinkman, the software engineer from South Carolina, now knows that he has royal blood running through his veins. His friends are having a lot of fun with this information. They are bowing down in his presence and addressing him as "your majesty." Brinkman, for his part, has joined the King Richard III Society, a group that brings together the king's relatives, and is dedicated to improving the king's reputation, which William Shakespeare stained in the play that he wrote about the king.[1]

Imagine what it would be like to be David Brinkman! One minute you're nothing but an average and ordinary software engineer. The next minute you're a descendant of a king. In light of his new identity, I wonder if he stands a bit taller when he walks into a room. I wonder if he gets any additional respect at work or at home. I wonder if he treats his wife like a queen. I wonder if he will name his next dog Prince! Imagine what it would be like to learn that you have royal blood running through your veins.

Something similar is going on in today's scripture from Matthew 22. As you recall, some of the religious leaders wanted to trap Jesus. They wanted to get him to say something that he'd regret. They said to him, "Is it lawful to pay taxes to the emperor, or not?" If Jesus said "yes," then he could be accused of siding with the Romans, and thereby turning his back on his own people, who were living under Roman occupation. If Jesus said, "No, it is not lawful to pay taxes to the emperor," then the Romans could accuse him of insurrection and arrest him for a crime against the state. Either answer was problematic. Saying "yes" ran the risk of being called a traitor. Saying "no" ran the risk of being called a political troublemaker. So how did the wise rabbi answer their trick question?

Before giving his answer, Jesus asked to see the coin used to pay the tax. "Whose head is this," he asked, "and whose title?" They all knew that the coin was not a Jewish coin but a Roman coin. The image on the coin did not belong to some hero of Jewish history. It was not the face of Abraham, Moses, David, or Ruth. Rather, the image on the coin belonged to a foreigner, the emperor of Rome, a constant reminder to the Jews that their land had been overrun by a foreign military power that ruled their lives with an iron fist and threatened crucifixion to anyone who stepped out of line. The image on that coin did not fill them with pride but with anger. It did not recall their storied past, but served as a painful reminder of the Roman occupation of their land.

Archeologists have unearthed some of these coins and they tell us that the image on the coin belonged to Tiberius

Caesar, emperor of Rome during the life of Jesus. The title on the coin said, "Tiberius Caesar, son of the divine Augustus," which meant Caesar Augustus, his father. As a result, that little coin made a big statement — political as well as religious — demanding your loyalty every time you used it — the emperor is the Son of God, there is no other.

No faithful Jew would ever willingly call Caesar a god or Tiberius "Son of God." Such statements flew in the face of their most cherished belief: "Hear, O Israel, the Lord our God, the Lord alone" (Deuteronomy 6:4).

What then did Jesus mean when he said, "Give to the emperor the things that are the emperor's, and give to God the things that are God's"? While some people think that Jesus was promoting a compartmentalized approach to life and faith, I think his words are more complicated than that. Can anyone really believe that Jesus, loyal Jew that he was, was placing Caesar on a par with God?

No, he was not suggesting that we divide our loyalties into neat little bundles, placing our loyalty to Caesar over here and our loyalty to God over here. Rather than urging us to divide our loyalties, Jesus invites us to *prioritize* our loyalties.

When Jesus asked, "Whose head is this and whose title?", he was asking about the image stamped on the coin. That is the explicit question he asked. But there was also an implicit question hanging in the air, one of which we all need to be reminded from time to time.

Writing way back in the third century AD, a church theologian by the name of Tertullian offered this interpretation of Jesus' words:

> *Render to Caesar, Caesar's image, which is on the coin, and render to God, God's image, which is stamped on every man and woman.*[2]

Remember, you and I have been created in the image of God. We have God's image stamped on us the way that old coin bore the stamp of Caesar. You might even say that we have royal blood running through our veins, the way that software engineer, David Brinkman, has royal blood running through his. If this is so, how can we be loyal to the royal that is within us? How can we render to God what is God's?

Certainly not by compartmentalizing, that's for sure, which tends to minimize and even trivialize God's exclusive claim on our lives. Remember what the scriptures teach us — that everything we have in life has been loaned to us by God: the air we breathe, the water we drink, the food we harvest from the land, the money we earn and spend. We don't really own any of these things; they have simply been loaned to us for whatever time we have here on earth. They have been entrusted to us.

The church has a word to describe this understanding of life and that word is stewardship. Unfortunately, we tend to define that word much too narrowly. We think of it only in terms of the annual fund raising effort at the church. But to be stewards of the riches of God is about so much more:

- It has to do with the way that we care for the earth, so that hopefully we do not threaten death to the planet entrusted to our care.
- It has to do with the quality of our relationships with loved ones.
- It has to do with the way we treat neighbors as well as strangers, each of them also created in the image of God.
- It has to do with the care of our own bodies, as we remember that our bodies are temples of the Holy Spirit.
- It has to do with the way we spend our time, whether we are wasting time, or making time for something enduring.
- And it has to do with the way we manage and spend our money. Whether we hoard it and keep it all to ourselves, or give away a pittance, or whether we invest it in places that would make God proud — including the church and

its mission, says a lot about us and our relationship with God.

I recall reading about a minister who liked to conduct what he called "spiritual checkups." Just as your doctor urges you to have an annual checkup to monitor your physical health, so this minister conducted checkups to monitor the spiritual health of his members. By asking his members a series of questions, he could determine whether or not they were spiritually mature and alive. He asked:

Why is Sunday worship important to you?

Do you have a daily discipline of praying and reading scripture?

Do you volunteer your time to the church or community?

If someone were to ask you how much of your income you give to God and the work of the church, could you name the percentage? In this way, the minister was able to help his members discern their spiritual health.

Similarly, in an essay called "Household Economics," professor Sharon Daloz Parks writes about an Old Testament professor who when addressing a group of clergy and laity said, "I'm really not interested in your 'story of faith.' I want to know about your 'story with money.' And someone else has written, "Show me your checkbook and I will tell you what you believe."[3]

Anybody can render to Caesar. It's just a matter of paying your taxes. But to render to God, the one who has stamped a royal and heavenly image on our lives — that's a much bigger challenge that is only possible because of the example of Jesus Christ and the encouragement of the Holy Spirit.

According to legend, before knights went off to fight the Crusades, they would receive the Sacrament of Baptism. They would wade into the river and immerse themselves under the water. However, many of the knights did something curious. Although they immersed themselves head to toe, they held their right arm high above the water, the arm with which they held their sword. It was as if they were saying,

"You can have all of me, Jesus, except this arm that holds my sword. I can't give that over to the Prince of Peace, since I will need to call upon that sword in battle." They were living according to a compartmentalized view of life.

Remember, like David Brinkman, the software engineer from South Carolina, we have royal blood running through our veins. Therefore, there is nothing that we should withhold from Christ, for we have been stamped with God's own image.

Amen.

---

1. Jeff Hampton, "DNA Shows Descendants with Ties to King Richard III" in *The Virginian-Pilot*, April 26, 2005.
2. As quoted by Susan Grove Eastman, in *Feasting on the Word*, Year A, Vol. 4 (Louisville: Westminster John Knox Press, 2011), p. 193.
3. Sharon Daloz Parks, "Household Economics" in *Practicing Our Faith*, Dorothy C. Bass, ed. (San Francisco: Jossey-Bass Publishers, 1997), p. 46.

Proper 25 / Pentecost 21 / Ordinary Time 30
Matthew 22:34-46

The Rule of Love

Teacher, which commandment in the law is the greatest?
— Matthew 22:36

In one of her books, the eloquent Episcopal priest, Barbara Brown Taylor, wrote these words about the Bible: "My relationship with the Bible is a marriage, not a romance, and one I am willing to work on in all the usual ways."[1] What she meant, of course, was that her relationship with the Bible was like any other serious relationship; it included good days as well as challenging days, days of clarity and days of confusion, days of joy and even days of dread. Everybody has favorite parts of the Bible, verses that make our spirits soar. But what do you do with those troubling parts of scripture, which, unfortunately, certain people like to wield like a club?

For example, last December, just as we Christians were preparing to celebrate the birth of the Christ child, a Baptist minister from Tempe, Arizona gained a lot of notoriety by preaching a sermon against homosexuals. Not only did he declare that "no queers or homos would be allowed in his church," he also proposed a way to rid the world of AIDS. Quoting from Leviticus 20:13 which says, "If a man lies with a male as with a woman, both of them have committed an abomination; they shall be put to death," the minister said that the way to get rid of AIDS was to kill all gay people.[2] It's right there in the Bible, part of the Law of Moses.

It goes without saying that reasonable Christian people will disagree about the place of gays and lesbians in society and, yes, even in the church. If we were to ask twelve people in this congregation what they think about gays and lesbians, we would get at least thirteen or fourteen opinions. It is, after all, one of the hot button social issues of our day. But how many of us would agree with that Baptist minister from Arizona who believes that all gay people should be put to death? Hopefully not many of us, but on what basis do we disagree, since he quotes from the Bible to support his opinion?

That's what I want to talk about today, not so much about homosexuality but about the Bible and how we make sense of it in the midst of this modern world in which God has put us.

As is true of most Christian churches, the Presbyterian Church has had a long colorful history trying to make sense of the Bible and then interpret and apply it to life. Admittedly, this has been a source of tension within the denomination. In 1976, some thoughtful Presbyterians formed a task force to seek answers to a vexing question: "Why do Presbyterians fight with each other so much?" Perhaps, you've heard the old joke, which says that wherever a member of the Scottish Macleod family went, a Presbyterian church was sure to follow. And wherever a second member of the Macleod family went, a *second* Presbyterian Church was sure to follow! Unfortunately, disputes, disagreements, and even schisms seem to be deeply embedded in our Presbyterian DNA.

A task force was appointed in 1976 to find out why. They decided to interview all living past Moderators of the Presbyterian Church, as well as members of the General Assembly staff and other church leaders. When they had finished their research, they came to this conclusion: "The most prevalent cause of conflict among Presbyterians is related to widely differing views of the ways the Old and New Testament are accepted, interpreted, and applied." Then the task force added, "It is our opinion that until our church examines this problem, our denomination will continue to be impeded in its mission and ministry, or we will spiral into a destructive schism."[3]

Ironically, what happened next was not schism, but reunion! In the early 1980s the two largest branches of the Presbyterian Church in this country, the so-called Northern and Southern churches, reunited 130 years after a major schism that had been caused by the Civil War and different ways of reading the Bible with regard to slavery. In preparing for reunion, each branch of the church created a document that spelled out what they believed about the authority of the Bible and how to interpret and apply it.

Just as people who are dating want to know something about each other before getting too serious, so these two churches before reuniting wanted to know what the other thought about the Bible and how to apply it to day-to-day living.

These statements are wonderfully written, articulate, and carefully capture what Presbyterians think and believe about the Bible. Each statement is twenty pages or more, far too lengthy to discuss in detail in any one sermon, so for today, if you'll allow me to do so, I want to highlight several points.

Maybe it will surprise you to hear this Yankee preacher say what I am about to say — that I actually prefer the document created by the Southern Church more than the one created by the Northern Church in which I grew up!

The document produced by the Southern Church is called *Presbyterian Understanding and Use of Holy Scripture* and it lays out a number of important guidelines. One of those guidelines affirms The Centrality of Jesus Christ. Another way to state this guideline is to ask: "Do we worship the Bible, or do we worship the Lord Jesus Christ, to whom the scriptures point and in whom they find their finest and fullest expression?" The guideline states:

> *No understanding of what scripture teaches us to believe and do can be correct that ignores the central and primary revelation of God's will through Jesus Christ.*[4]

Another guideline affirms The Interpretation of Scripture by Scripture. In other words, you can't cherry pick one verse here and another there and claim that those verses, isolated from the message of the Bible as a whole, constitute God's will and God's truth.

Yet another guideline is called The Rule of Love, and as you can see, I have borrowed this phrase for the title of this sermon. This is at the heart of what I would say to that Baptist minister from Arizona:

> *The fundamental expression of God's will is the twofold commandment to love God and neighbor, and all interpretations of the Bible are to be judged by the question whether they offer and support the love given and commanded by God... Any interpretation of scripture is wrong that separates or sets in opposition love for God and love for fellow human being, including both love expressed in individual relations and in human community. No interpretation of scripture is correct that leads to or supports contempt for any individual or group of people, either within or outside of the church.*[5]

Speaking of the twofold commandment to love God and neighbor, we heard that described for us in this morning's scripture. According to Matthew, the Pharisees sent a lawyer to put Jesus to the test. Actually, he was more of a Bible scholar than a modern-day lawyer. He was an expert in the law of Moses. "Teacher," he said to Jesus, "which commandment in the law is the greatest?"

By the way, this Bible scholar was not just thinking of the Ten Commandments. Jewish scholars who counted the laws of Moses came up with 613 commandments scattered throughout the Hebrew Bible. That's the test he put before Jesus! "Which of all of these 613 is the greatest?"

To answer, Jesus drew one commandment from the book of Deuteronomy: "You shall love the Lord your God with all your heart, and with all your soul and with all your mind"

(Deuteronomy 6:5). Jesus said, "This is the greatest and the first commandment." Then he drew another from the book of Leviticus, "You shall love your neighbor as yourself" (Leviticus 19:18). In summary he said, "On these two commandments, hang all the law and the prophets."

According to Professor Tom Long, Jesus' answer not only established his religious orthodoxy — who can argue with love God and love your neighbor as yourself? — it also challenged the Bible scholar and all like him who think that religion is primarily about keeping the rules. It's as if the Bible scholar says, "We have 613 rules here; now which rule is the most important?" According to Professor Long, "What Jesus claims is that the whole law is about love, not rules, about really loving God and one's neighbor, not about figuring out how to avoid stepping on cracks in the legal sidewalk."[6]

Because Jesus understood the law to be love-based rather than rules-based, he did all sorts of things throughout his ministry that seemingly broke the rules:
- He reached out and touched a leper, even though the rules said, "Keep away from people like that."
- He healed on the Sabbath day, even though the rules prevented it. "The Sabbath was made for us," he said, "not us for the Sabbath."
- He ate and drank with tax collectors and sinners, even though the rules discouraged it.
- He befriended foreigners like Samaritans, even though they played by a different set of rules than did the Jews.
- If Jesus was here today, I am pretty sure he would sit down to eat with his Muslim neighbor and find some reason to praise his neighbor's faith as he once praised the faith of a Roman centurion.
- And I would be willing to bet that if Jesus was here today, he would willingly bake a cake or shoot photographs for a gay couple on their wedding day, because love rather than rule-keeping is at the heart of his faith.

"Love God and love your neighbor as yourself," he said. "Keep only these, and you will find that you are obeying all the others" (The Living Bible).

Amen.

---

1. Barbara Brown Taylor, *The Preaching Life* (Boston: Cowley Publications, 1993), p. 56.
2. "Pastor Calls for Killing Gays to End AIDS" in *USA Today*, December 6, 2014.
3. Jack Rogers, *Reading the Bible and the Confessions: The Presbyterian Way* (Louisville: Geneva Press, 1999), p. 14.
4. Presbyterian Understanding and Use of Holy Scripture (1983) (Louisville: Published by The Office of the General Assembly, 1992), p. 17.
5. *Ibid.*, pp. 19-20.
6. Thomas G. Long, *Matthew*, in the Westminster Bible Companion Series (Louisville: Westminster John Knox Press, 1997), pp. 254-255.

Reformation Sunday
John 8:31-36

The Word Above All Earthly Powers

If you continue in my word, you are truly my disciples, and you will know the truth and the truth will set you free.
— John 8:31-32

Recently, I came across a list of the 100 most influential people of the last 1,000 years. First on the list is Johannes Gutenberg, inventor of the printing press with moveable type. Following right on his heels and coming in at number three, is one of my all-time faith heroes, a Catholic priest by the name of Martin Luther.[1]

According to tradition, exactly 500 years ago this Tuesday, on the eve of All Saints Day in 1517, Luther nailed his 95 theses on the door of the university chapel in Wittenberg, Germany. He did so to protest a series of practices in the Roman Catholic Church, particularly the sale of indulgences, money people would pay the church for the forgiveness of sins. Although Luther did not set out to create a new denomination, his efforts, combined with the efforts of Zwingli, Calvin, Knox, Bucer, and others, led to what we have come to call the Protestant Reformation, the monumental changes that took place in religion, society, and politics in sixteenth-century Europe. We celebrate that heritage today!

We remember Luther for many reasons. He was a Catholic priest who married a nun, thereby paving the way for married clergy. He was the author of a number of hymns including the ever popular, "A Mighty Fortress Is Our God." He was a university professor of theology who taught that salvation is not earned by good works but comes as a free gift of God's grace through faith in Jesus Christ. He is the namesake of the Lutheran Church, the Protestant denomination that followed in his footsteps. Perhaps most important of all, Luther was an avid translator of the Bible. He believed that the scriptures did not belong exclusively to church professionals, so he translated the Bible from Latin into his local language, German, thereby making the scriptures accessible to anyone who could read. Thanks to Johannes Gutenberg, inventor of the printing press with moveable type, copies of Luther's Bible translations were printed and then distributed far and wide, setting the stage for dramatic changes in church and society.

Luther held ideas about the Bible that were both unusual and beautiful. According to church historian Martin Marty, Luther ...

> *... held controversial ideas about who wrote Ecclesiastes, Jude, Proverbs, and even parts of Genesis.... As for the book of Revelation, he wrote that his spirit could not make its way into it... Though the brother of Jesus wrote the Letter of James, Luther found it "right strawy," a book which contradicted the central Pauline teaching that one is saved by grace without the works of the law.*[2]

On the other hand, Luther spoke of the scriptures with beauty and reverence. He called the Bible, "the manger in which Christ lay, the swaddling clothes he wore," and said that Christ is the "central point of the circle around which everything else in the Bible revolves."[3] Professor Marty tells us that Luther preferred the gospel of John to the other three because John's gospel helps readers *have* faith in Christ, while the other gospels tell stories *about* Christ.[4]

And that brings us to today's gospel text from John chapter eight, where Jesus said, "If you continue in my word, you are truly my disciples, and you will know the truth and the truth will set you free." In this single sentence, John brought together two of the great words of his gospel — *word* and *truth*. Let's consider them one by one.

As you may recall, John began his gospel with the beautiful and soaring words of his prologue, words we often read in church at Christmas:

In the beginning was the Word, and the Word was with God, and the Word was God. He was in the beginning with God. All things came into being through him, and without him not one thing came into being. What has come into being in him was life, and the life was the light of all people. The light shines in the darkness and the darkness did not overcome it.

— John 1:1-5

A few verses later John adds, "And the Word became flesh and lived among us…" (John 1:14). What an amazing way to talk about Jesus coming into the world. The Word became flesh… and, as Eugene Peterson puts it in his apt paraphrase of the New Testament, "The Word became flesh… and moved into the neighborhood."

This truth is incredibly important because it helps us to know what God is like. Whenever we ponder the mysterious nature of God:
- when we wonder why bad things happen to good people,
- or think about good and evil in the world,
- or wonder what God would want us to do in a given situation, we can fall back on this verse. "The Word became flesh and lived among us."

In other words, God has chosen to enter the neighborhood of our world by taking on human flesh in the person of Jesus of Nazareth. This is what we mean when we speak about the doctrine of the Incarnation. God has chosen to live as one of us. Because of this, whenever we look at Jesus — the Word of God Incarnate — his life, teachings, miracles, death, and resurrection, we get a better glimpse of what God is really like.

When Luther summarized the changes that took place in the church at the time of the Reformation, he credited everything to the word. He wrote:

> *I simply taught, preached, and wrote God's word; otherwise I did nothing. And while I slept or drank beer with my friends, the word so greatly weakened the papacy that no prince or emperor ever inflicted such losses upon it. I did nothing; the Word did everything."*[5]

No wonder Luther wrote about "That Word above all earthly powers" in his most famous hymn.

Some years ago, the former president of Princeton Seminary was traveling in Eastern Europe and arrived at the border of Romania. The customs agent asked President Gillespie this unusual series of questions: "Do you have any drugs? Do you have any pornography? Do you have any Bibles?" Although those three things are very different from one another, they do have this in common: Each has the power to disrupt society and turn things upside down, as Martin Luther learned hundreds of years before.

The other great word in the vocabulary of John's gospel is the word *truth*. John used this word some twenty times in his gospel story but nowhere more dramatically than in the Upper Room in Jerusalem. Jesus was preparing his disciples for his upcoming glorification on the cross. Within hours he would be arrested, tried, and crucified. He told them what would lay ahead. He said, "In my Father's house there are many dwelling places... I go to prepare a place for you." A moment later he added, "And you know the place where I am going."

"Lord, we do not know where you are going," said Thomas, one of the twelve, "how can we know the way?"

"I am the way, the truth, and the life," said Jesus, "no one comes to the Father except through me."

Contained within that brief phrase is a summary of John's theology about Jesus. "I am the *life*," said Jesus, the only life really worth living.

"I am the *way*," he said, in other words, the way to God. And this way is none other than the way of the cross. As early as the first chapter of John's gospel, John the Baptist pointed to Jesus and said, "Here is the Lamb of God, who takes away the sins of the world" (John 1:29). Later in the gospel Jesus would say, "When I am lifted up (and by this he means lifted up on the cross), when I am lifted up, I will draw all people to myself" (John 12:32-33). He said this, wrote John, to indicate the kind of death he was to die. Clearly, the way of Jesus is the way of the cross. So when he said, "I am the way," he invited us to follow that way, the way of the cross, in terms of service and self-sacrifice.

Joseph Sittler, who used to teach theology at the University of Chicago, was once attending a conference at a Roman Catholic convent. The convent sisters went to chapel four times each day for prayer and meditation. There they would meditate upon the large crucifix hanging over the altar. Professor Sittler said to himself:

> *Is there any other image in the history of the world that could survive such constant gazing? What other form could absorb all of the worries and apprehensions heaped upon it? Throughout history, the figure of the crucified one has been at the center of devotional gravity, the center of human pain and torment.*[6]

Then Jesus said what is, perhaps, the most important word of all: "I am the *truth*." Please notice that this truth does not find its form in a doctrine or a proposition. Rather, this truth resides in a person! This is the truth about God to which the way of the cross points. I am aware of no other religion in the world that holds up a crucified leader and says — if you want to know what God is really like, then look at this cross, this symbol for suffering and sacrifice, for here on this cross you will see the truth about God which no other religion captures in the same way.

If you live your life by following Jesus' example of service and self-sacrifice, then you will know the truth about life and about God, and that truth will set you free.

In one of his books, Professor Tom Long wrote about Mr. and Mrs. Williams, a deeply religious couple, who adopted four children and hoped to adopt at least one more. The types of children the Williams adopted were the type that the adoption agency termed "hard to adopt." You see, one of their children, a son, is severely retarded; the other three have major birth defects. "Our children are our greatest joy," said Mrs. Williams. "Caring for them is what we have been put on this earth to do."[7]

Not only is Christ the way, the truth, and the life, but if you will permit me this little play on words, he is also "the way to the truth about life." Knowing this truth will set you free.

Amen.

---

1. The Biography Channel, Arts and Entertainment Network.
2. Martin Marty, *Martin Luther* (New York: Penguin Group Publishers, 2004), p. 84.
3. *Ibid.*
4. *Ibid.*, p. 85.
5. *Ibid.*, p. 86.
6. Joseph Sittler, *Gravity and Grace* (Minneapolis: Augsburg Publishing House, 1986), pp. 33-34.
7. Thomas G. Long, *The Witness of Preaching* (Louisville: Westminster John Knox Press, 1989), p. 168.

All Saints Day
Matthew 5:1-12

Blessed to Be Among the Company of Mourners

Blessed are those who mourn, for they will be comforted.
— Matthew 5:4

Recently I conducted four funerals in four weeks and by the end of the month I was emotionally and spiritually exhausted. It's hard enough to conduct a funeral for a stranger, far more so for a friend. And these people were my friends, friends with whom I had attended parties, shared meals, and enjoyed a laugh or a good joke. At the reception following the fourth of those funerals, I leaned over to someone and only half jokingly whispered, "If there is one more funeral at this church any time soon, it might just be for me!"

Although I didn't realize it at the time, I was caught up in my own grief. As the "professional minister," who is supposed to help others with their grief, I was wandering through a grief-filled wilderness of my own. One of our members, a retired physician, sensed my sorrow and sent me a beautiful and comforting email. Here in part is what he wrote to me (he has given me permission to share):

> *I've been thinking of the personal effect these continuing losses of your parishioners must have on you and your wife. I assume such sorrow is offset by the joy of the baptisms and marriages you perform and the comfort you provide to the sick and needy by your hospital visits and wise counsel. It must still at times be difficult for you. In my 43 years of medical practice, I experienced such similar sorrow and internal conflict when witnessing the*

depth of human suffering and the loss of patients, many of whom I had known for years.

The doctor's email did two things for me. First, it reminded me that he and I, in fact all of us together, are part of what Nicholas Wolterstorff once called "the company of mourners." Wolterstorff, a minister of the Christian Reformed Church, lost a son who was only 25 years old. The son had been mountain climbing in Austria when he slipped on a narrow mountain trail and fell to his death. Some time after his son's death, Wolterstorff wrote a book called *Lament for a Son*, in which he described and explored the depth of his own grief.[1]

- "The pain of the *no more*," he wrote, "far outweighs the gratitude of the *once was*" (p. 13).
- "It's hard enough to bury our parents," he wrote. "But that we expect. Our parents belong to our past; our children belong to our future. We do not visualize our future without them. How can I bury my son, my future…He was meant to bury me!" (p. 16).
- "Death has made my son special. He is special in my grieving. When I give thanks, I mention all five of my children; when I lament I mention only him. Wounded love is special love, special in its wound. Now I think of him every day; before, I did not. Of the five, only he has a grave" (p. 59).

You get the sense, don't you, of the breadth and depth of that father's pain? You wonder whether he will ever make his way through his wilderness of grief. Yet, he wrote the book to try to share his pain with others. In the preface he says, "I have written this book in the hope that it will be of help to others who find themselves with us in the company of mourners."

The company of mourners — what a telling phrase that is! While grief is always private and personal, it is also a common experience that comes to us all. Sooner or later every one of us suffers some significant loss. As a result, we are all members of the company of mourners. How important to affirm that today, on All Saints' Sunday, the day the church calendar sets aside to remember those who have passed from this life into the life to come, those known to us as well as those who died before we were even born. We believe that they now surround us as a great cloud of witnesses — family, friends, and strangers — whose lives we remember and whose deaths we continue to grieve because we also belong to the company of mourners.

The other thing that the doctor's email did was to remind me of the truth of Jesus' beatitude, "Blessed are those who mourn, for they will be comforted." In the midst of my grief, the doctor's email was a great source of comfort to me as in his own compassionate way he ministered to the minister. Talk about the priesthood of all believers — what a wonderful example!

We live in a time when religion has become a highly individualistic thing. Believing is popular, but belonging to a religious institution like the church is not. As a result, faith has become a private matter for many people. Yet, to this privatization of religion, the New Testament offers a stern challenge:

- "Love one another," said Jesus. "Just as I have loved you, you also should love one another" (John 13:34).
- "Bear one another's burdens," wrote the apostle Paul, "and in this way you will fulfill the law of Christ" (Galatians 6:2).
- "Blessed be the God and Father of our Lord Jesus Christ," wrote Paul, "who consoles us in all our affliction, so that we may console those who are in any affliction with the consolation with which we ourselves are consoled by God" (2 Corinthians 1:3-4).

Can you see how the Christian faith invites us, and even *compels* us, to comfort one another, reaching out to those who suffer and grieve and mourn? And miracle of miracles, when people experience the comfort of others, often they remember the God of all comfort who comforts us in all our afflictions.

When the Reverend William Sloan Coffin lost his son in a tragic car accident, he said that while the words of the Bible are true, grief renders them unreal.[2] But that was only for a time. The more his friends reached out to him with love and care, the more he began to experience the comfort that they offered until eventually those timeless, truthful words of scripture came alive for him once again. These are some of the words that consoled him:

- "Cast your burden on the Lord and he will sustain you" (Psalm 55:22).
- "Weeping may linger for the night, but joy comes with the morning" (Psalm 30:5).
- "For you have delivered my soul from death, and my feet from falling, so that I may walk before God in the light of life" (Psalm 56:13).
- "I have said this to you, so that in me you may have peace. In the world you face persecution and tribulation. But take courage; I have conquered the world!" (John 16:33).
- "The light shines in the darkness, and the darkness did not overcome it" (John 1:5).[3]

"Blessed are those who mourn," said Jesus, "for they will be comforted." But by whom? Don't you wonder why Jesus never tells us who will provide the source of that comfort? That's because it can be different for each of us. For some, the comfort may come in the form of a plate of chocolate chip cookies; for others it comes as a sympathy note in the mail. For others it takes the form of a friend who sits with you and holds your hand as you make your way through that dark night of the soul. For others, the comfort may come through scripture, prayer, or that peace of God that surpasses all understanding. But sooner or later we begin to feel it — the comfort that comes to those who mourn. And when that happens, we find that we are blessed, just as Jesus has promised, and we rediscover the happiness and joy of life. "For weeping may linger for the night, but joy comes in the morning" (Psalm 30:5).

Amen.

---

1. Nicholas Wolterstorff, *Lament for a Son* (Grand Rapids: William B. Eerdmans Publishing Company, 1987).
2. William Sloan Coffin, "Alex's Death" in *A Chorus of Witnesses*, Thomas G. Long and Cornelius Plantinga Jr. eds. (Grand Rapids: William B. Eerdmans Publishing Company, 1994), p. 264.
3. *Ibid.*, p. 266.

Proper 26 / Pentecost 22 / Ordinary Time 31
Matthew 23:1-12

Practicing What We Preach

The scribes and the Pharisees sit on Moses' seat; therefore, do whatever they teach you and follow it; but do not do as they do, for they do not practice what they teach.
— Matthew 23:2-3

In today's scripture from Matthew, Jesus accused the scribes and the Pharisees of hypocrisy. And he did not do it just once, but numerous times. Indeed, throughout Matthew's gospel, Jesus spoke more often about "hypocrites" than he did about "prayer." I was surprised to discover that! He spoke about hypocrisy twelve times in Matthew, six of them in Matthew 23 alone. By way of contrast, Jesus spoke about prayer in Matthew a mere nine times. This is not to minimize the importance of prayer. It merely suggests that hypocrisy was a huge issue in Jesus' day, just as it is today.

Do you know what hypocrites are? Originally the word was a term from the ancient Greek theater. An actor would appear on stage wearing a large grinning mask and would quote humorous lines, causing the audience to laugh. The actor would disappear backstage, put on a frowning mask and then reappear quoting somber lines that would cause the audience to sigh and moan. That actor with his two faces was called a *hypocritos*, one who wears a mask.[1]

Therefore, hypocrites are people who put on a false face. They pretend to be something they are not. They are people whose deeds don't match their words, whose conduct is inconsistent with their creed, and whose actions are out of step with their alleged beliefs.

We don't have to look very hard to find them — do we? — especially in the areas of politics and religion? Do you remember Eliot Spitzer? He was attorney general and later governor of the state of New York. As attorney general Spitzer led a zealous campaign against the commercial sexual exploitation of women, he received high praise from women's rights groups for doing so. However, we have since learned that during that same time, Spitzer himself was hiring the services of a $1,000 per hour prostitute.

Dennis Hastert has been in the news lately. During President Clinton's tawdry extramarital affair with Monica Lewinsky, Congressman Hastert voted to impeach Clinton. Later as Speaker of the House, he twice tried to get the House to pass a constitutional amendment to ban same sex marriage. But now, some young men have accused Hastert of sexually abusing them when they were members of the high school wrestling team that he coached.[2]

Many politicians on both sides of the political aisle love to remind us that the Judeo-Christian tradition lies at the heart of our nation. They say that we need to make faith a bigger part of our national life, a statement with which I totally agree. But when the pope calls climate change a global problem and urges us to action based on his reading of the Bible's story of creation, these same politicians tell the pope to stick to the business of religion, as if the care of earth is something other than a religious issue.

Then there's Bill Cosby, the popular comedian and TV actor. Perhaps his most endearing role was as the wise and loving dad on *The Cosby Show*. It was the number one show on American TV for five years in a row in the 1990s, making Cosby into something like "America's Dad." But now he has admitted to drugging multiple women before raping them.

I could go on and on, but I think you get the point. You don't have to look far to find examples of hypocrisy in our world today. But that's out there. What about in here? Jesus, you recall, was not criticizing secular people, but some of the most religious people of his day. Please notice that he did not criticize them for the message they taught. Indeed, he felt their message was very important. He said to this disciples, "Do whatever they teach you and follow it." But then, he quickly added, "Do not do as they do, for they do not practice what they teach." In other words, they were people whose deeds didn't match their words, whose conduct was inconsistent with their creed, and whose actions were out of step with their alleged beliefs. No wonder he called them hypocrites, which causes me to wonder whether he might find any hypocrites among us!

If I've heard it once, I've heard it a thousand times. Maybe you've heard it too. When you ask people, "Why don't you go to church?" they often answer by saying, "The reason I don't go to church is because the church is full of hypocrites." Have you ever heard anything like that? I thought so.

Do you know what? By and large, that criticism is correct. The church does have its fair share of hypocrites. Just listen to this comment:

> *In this church are mingled many hypocrites who have nothing of Christ but his name and outward appearance. There are very many ambitious, greedy, envious persons, evil speakers, and some of quite an unclean life.*[3]

Do you know who said that? Not some outsider who never darkened the door of the church. Rather, the pioneer of Presbyterian theology: John Calvin. Listen to this comment:

> *When outsiders say, "The church is just a bunch of hypocrites," we admit that we are a gathering of sinners, some of whom are hypocrites. We are no more embarrassed by this than by the observation that hospitals are full of sick people. Long ago Jesus was criticized for receiving sinners and eating with them. He still does that, every time the church gathers.*[4]

Do you know who said that? Not some outsider but Methodist Bishop William Willimon, the former dean of the chapel at Duke University.

To be honest about it, hypocrisy in the church is not necessarily a bad thing. It can be a hopeful thing if it leads us to change and grow. Let me suggest two ways that this can be so.

Suggestion number one comes from the Canadian theologian Douglas John Hall. In one of his books he writes, "We should never underestimate the capacity of the human mind, especially the minds of children and adolescents, to sense contradiction. It is probably the greatest hope of the race, humanly speaking."[5]

In other words, children and youth can spot hypocrisy from a mile away. Best selling author Annie Dillard recalls her religious upbringing in the Shadyside Presbyterian Church in Pittsburgh. What she found most disturbing was the hypocrisy of her parents who forced her to attend church while they never attended themselves.[6] It didn't take her long to figure out that her parents did not practice what they preached.

I wonder how many of us have ever done something similar with our children or grandchildren — urging them to do something but then not doing it ourselves.

Encouraging them to believe something, but then not believing it ourselves. Telling them to love something or someone but then acting in ways that deny that love in our own lives. Children can spot hypocrisy from a mile away and we owe it to them and ourselves to make sure that our actions match our words.

Suggestion number two comes from a delightful book called *Channel Markers,* written by Presbyterian minister Bill Enright. In the book, he tells of the day he arrived in Indianapolis to begin his work as the minister of Second Presbyterian.

He began his work at that church on April 1 — April Fools' Day — a rather ominous beginning if ever there was one. As he pulled into the driveway of his new home, four people walked out to meet him.

"Who are you and what are you doing here?" asked one of them.

"I'm Bill Enright," he replied. "I'm the new minister of Second Presbyterian."

"Are you sure about that?"

"Not as sure as I was five minutes ago," he replied.

At this point Bill began to think that perhaps these were the four members of the congregation who had voted *against* calling him as the next minister. Eventually, the four men explained that there had been an armed robbery in that neighborhood a few days before, and they wanted to make sure that Bill was not the robber.

Later, Enright would say to himself, "Bill, if you are going to survive in Indianapolis, you'll have to be on your best behavior, because these Hoosiers appear to have difficulty distinguishing between robbers and preachers!"[7]

He calls the final chapter of his book, "Living As If God Were Your Only Audience," and in it he makes the case for living with sincerity and integrity, not so much to impress others, but simply to be true to God, who is watching every breath you take, every move you make, whether you realize it or not. As an example, Enright writes about charitable giving. He says:

> *Disciples of Jesus Christ give generously, but not for a tax write off. Disciples of Jesus give away all the money they can in order to make the presence of God's kingdom a reality in this world. Disciples of Jesus write big checks because the account from which they draw is the ocean of God's generosity.*[8]

What a marvelous example of living with sincerity and integrity, which are the opposites of hypocrisy. It's but a single example of practicing what we preach. I know you can give many more examples of your own by the way you live your life.

Amen.

---

1. Charles R. Swindoll, *Improving Your Serve: The Art of Unselfish Living* (Waco: Word Books, 1981), p. 117.
2. Jonathan Capehart, "Nothing Gay About Hastert Hypocrisy" in *The Washington Post*, June 7, 2005.
3. John Calvin, *Calvin's Institutes: A New Compend*, Hugh T. Kerr, ed. (Louisville: Westminster John Knox Press, 1989), p. 133.
4. William Willimon, *With Glad and Generous Hearts* (Nashville: Upper Room Books, 1986), p. 41.
5. Douglas John Hall, *Why Christian?* (Minneapolis: Fortress Press, 1998), p. 6.
6. Annie Dillard, *An American Childhood* (New York: Harper and Row Publishers, 1987), p. 196.
7. William G. Enright, *Channel Markers* (Louisville: Geneva Press, 2001), pp. 77-78.
8. *Ibid.*, p. 86.

Proper 27 / Pentecost 23 / Ordinary Time 32
Matthew 25:1-13

Are You Ready to Wait?

And while they went to buy it, the bridegroom came and those who were ready went with him into the wedding banquet.
— Matthew 25:10

Have you ever noticed how waiting — waiting for something or someone — can be either wonderful or dreadful? To a large degree the difference is determined by what you are waiting for. Waiting for your bride to come down the aisle of the church can be wonderful. Waiting to learn if your loved one has cancer can be dreadful. Waiting at the airport to meet your best friend can be wonderful; waiting for a root canal can be dreadful.

Waiting for a promotion — wonderful; waiting to see if you'll lose your job due to corporate downsizing — dreadful; and waiting to purchase your dream house — wonderful; waiting to be audited by the IRS is absolutely dreadful.

As you probably know, there is a lot of waiting that takes place in the church, and I'm not talking about waiting for the sermon to be over! Our waiting is much more meaningful than that —

We wait for a new heaven and a new earth.

We wait for God's kingdom to come on earth as it is in heaven, as we pray in the words of the Lord's Prayer.

When we celebrate Holy Communion we say that we proclaim the Lord's death until he comes again... and we are waiting for that day to come.

When we say the Apostles' Creed we affirm our belief in the one who will come to judge the quick and the dead.

Much of our waiting, therefore, is waiting for Christ to return to earth, something that the church calls the second coming. In one of his books, Marcus Borg points out that expectation about the second coming has been a part of Christian tradition since the very beginning. "Of the 27 books in the New Testament, 21 refer to the second coming."[1]

But what will it be like? Will it be a time of wonder or of dread? Some Christians associate the second coming of Christ with the end of the world, a great cosmic battle, or a horrific holocaust in which God will save a small remnant but destroy everything and everyone else. From my point of view, that idea is both nonsense and really bad theology. God created the world and pronounced it good. God loves the world and everyone and everything in it. God sent Christ into the world not to condemn the world, but in order that the world might be saved through him. God does not want to destroy the world but to redeem it and make things right.

Canadian theologian Douglas John Hall offers harsh words to those who believe that Christ will return only to destroy:

> *If the world does end, its end will have to be attributed in part to these simplifiers [of faith], who were more concerned for their own personal salvation than for the healing of creation. Because they wanted above all else to shield themselves from the world's brokenness, they could have no part of its mending.*[2]

So we wait for Christ to return, not to destroy the world but to redeem it, not to annihilate and obliterate but to set things right. We wait for him to finish the work he began in the manger in Bethlehem and even more importantly on the cross of Calvary.

But let's face it; waiting for Christ to return is difficult. After all, we Christians have been waiting for 2,000 years and his return seems no more imminent today than it did way back when. In fact, the longer the delay, the easier it is to lose hope that he will ever return at all. Edmund Steimle, a Lutheran minister, once wrote about Christ's delayed return in these words:

> *On the roof of the Riverside Church in New York is the figure of the angel Gabriel, his horn lifted to his mouth ready to give out a mighty blast to announce the second coming of our Lord in glory. Day after day he stands ready. Warmed by the summer sun, frozen by winter sleet, year after year goes by, but there is no mighty blast, not even a tentative toot.*[3]

"No mighty blast to announce the second coming in glory," writes Steimle, "not even a tentative toot." Instead, the sounds we hear most often are the discouraging shouts of the newspaper headlines:
- Radical ISIS group beheads women and children in Syria.
- College student abducted late at night. Police discover her body several weeks later.
- Racial tensions erupt following the shooting of a black man by a white police officer.
- Fighting between Israel and Palestine escalates following Israel's decision to close off access to the temple mount.

With news stories such as these, it's pretty easy to lose heart, grow discouraged, and give up hope. We may pray, "Thy kingdom come, on earth as it is in heaven," but in spite of our well-meaning prayers, God's kingdom seems no closer today than it did yesterday or last month or last year. No wonder we are tempted to toss in the towel, give up our hope for a better tomorrow, and call it quits.

But the New Testament won't let us do that and in its own prophetic way urges us to believe that "Christ has died. Christ is risen. Christ will come again," as we say in our

Communion liturgy. The challenge we face is how to live our lives in the meantime. And that brings us to the parable of the wise and foolish bridesmaids that we read a few moments ago. It's one of several parables about the return of Christ, which the gospel writer Matthew tells us one right after the next.

Some New Testament parables extol the virtue of watchfulness saying "Keep alert, for you do not know the day or hour when Christ will return." But this parable takes a different tack, urging us to be ready — not so much ready for his return but ready to wait — assuming his return will be delayed. The foolish bridesmaids are chastised not because they fail to watch and not because they fall asleep — all of them fall asleep, the wise as well as the foolish. Rather, they are chastised because they didn't bring enough lamp oil to keep their lamps burning during the bridegroom's delay.

Like a number of Jesus' parables, this one is best understood allegorically — things in the story represent other things. For example: the wedding banquet is a symbol for the kingdom of God, the bridegroom is clearly Jesus, and the bridegroom's midnight arrival suggests that the messiah will return at an unexpected time. But what does the oil symbolize? In the opinion of Professor Tom Long, the wise bridesmaids who brought with them extra oil "… represent those Christians who keep on doing the will of God even when the kingdom is delayed."[4] They keep their lamps burning even though the bridegroom is delayed in returning. As Jesus put it earlier in Matthew's gospel, "Let your light shine before others, so that they may see your good works and give glory to your Father in heaven" (Matthew 5:15).

So how do we do that? We do it by following the teachings that Jesus laid out earlier in the gospel story, especially those from the Sermon on the Mount. For example, we do it by embracing the future that Jesus imagines in his beatitudes:

- Blessed are the poor in spirit, for theirs is the kingdom

of heaven.
- Blessed are those who mourn, for they will be comforted.
- Blessed are the meek, for they will inherit the earth.
- Blessed are the peacemakers for they will be called children of God… and so on.

We keep on doing the will of God…by loving our enemies. "You have heard that it was said, 'You shall love your neighbor and hate your enemy,' " said Jesus, "but I say to you, 'Love your enemies and pray for those who persecute you.' "

We keep on doing the will of God… when we give money to the poor and pray the Lord's Prayer and fast and do all of them with humility and grace (Matthew 6:2, 5, 16).

We keep on doing the will of God… when we differentiate between loving God and loving money, remembering Jesus' words, "You cannot serve both God and wealth" (Matthew 6:24).

We keep on doing God's will… when we refuse to allow anxiety to control our lives. "Therefore, I tell you," said Jesus, "do not worry about your life, what you will eat or what you will drink, or about your body, what you will wear…Instead, strive first for the kingdom God and his righteousness, and all these things will be given to you as well" (Matthew 6:25, 33).

We keep on doing God's will… when we live by the golden rule, "doing to others as you would have them do to you; for this is the law and the prophets" (Matthew 7:12).

In short, we become the wise bridesmaids when we wait for Christ by living the kind of lives he, through his teachings, encourages us to live — letting our light shine before others, so that they may see our good works and give glory to God who is in heaven.

Amen.

1. Marcus J. Borg and N.T. Wright, *The Meaning of Jesus: Two Visions* (San Francisco: Harper San Francisco Publishers, 1999), p. 191.
2. Douglas John Hall, *Thinking the Faith* (Minneapolis: Fortress Press, 1991), p. 234.
3. Edmund A. Steimle, *Disturbed by Joy* (Philadelphia: Fortress Press, 1967), pp. 13-14.
4. Thomas G. Long, *Matthew* (Louisville: Westminster John Knox Press, 1997), p. 280.

Proper 28 / Pentecost 24 / Ordinary Time 33
Matthew 25:14-30

The Gospel We Preach

Master, I knew that you were a harsh man, reaping where you did not sow, and gathering where you did not scatter seed, so I was afraid and I went and hid your talent in the ground.
— Matthew 25:24

A number of years ago my wife and I and several of our friends went on a sailing vacation in the Caribbean. One day we went ashore on the island of Dominica, hired a taxi, and took a tour of that tropical paradise. While making small talk with the taxi driver, one of my friends casually mentioned that I was a minister. The cabbie looked me over in the rear view mirror and then in his island-flavored English he said to me, "You say you're a minister, mon. Well then, tell me: What kind of God do you believe in? What kind of gospel do you preach?"

The question caught me completely off guard! I was on vacation, after all, pondering palm trees, enjoying warm ocean breezes, and sipping tropical drinks in the setting sun. Talking theology was the last thing on my mind. So the cabbie's question came like a bolt out of the blue. What kind of God do you believe in? What kind of gospel do you preach?

The truth of the matter is that we all have some sort of image of what God is like. You have yours and I have mine, and while many of these images are helpful and wholesome, some of them are not.

In Tennessee Williams' provocative play, *The Night of the Iguana*, the lead character is a defrocked minister by the name of the Reverend Shannon. At one point in the play, he rants and raves about the kind of God many people believe in. He says:

> *[They think of God as]...this angry, petulant old man. I mean he's represented like a bad-tempered, childish, sick, peevish man — the sort of old man in a nursing home that's putting together a jigsaw puzzle and can't put it together and gets frustrated at it and kicks over the table. Yes, I tell you, they do that, all our theologies do it — accuse God of being a cruel, senile, delinquent.*[1]

William Barclay was one of the great biblical scholars of the twentieth century. A very faithful and devout teacher, with a God-given ability to communicate in the language of lay people, Barclay developed a reputation as something of a theological liberal. One day Barclay lost his daughter and son-in-law in a tragic boating accident. They had been sailing off the coast of Northern Ireland when a sudden storm came up and drowned both of them. After the funeral, Barclay received an anonymous letter from a woman who called herself a Christian. "I know why God killed your daughter," she wrote, "it was to save her from being corrupted by your heresies." Barclay couldn't reply to the letter because the woman hadn't signed her name. But he once remarked that if he could have answered, he would have said, "If that is the kind of God you believe in, then your God is my devil. The day my daughter was lost at sea, there was sorrow in the heart of God."[2]

More recently, I recall reading about a woman who grew up fearing God. It's one thing to possess a little bit of what the Bible calls "the fear of the Lord." That means awe, reverence, or respect for God, and that is a good thing. But this woman actually feared God. She once said to her minister:

> *You preach about God from the pulpit. Every week you encourage us to believe. You urge us to trust God with*

our lives. I wish I could do that, but I can't. The God I learned about as a child is not the friend you make him out to be. My God is an awesome figure who frightens me to death. In his presence, I feel more condemned than forgiven, more judged than loved. How can I put my trust in someone who makes me feel like that?[3]

Many people cling to such images of God — the angry old man in the nursing home, who kicks over the jigsaw puzzles we construct of our lives; the vengeful God of the self-righteous, who zaps those who think outside the bounds of a particular theology; the fearful God who frightens us to death.

All of these remind me of the one-talent man in today's scripture from Matthew. I have always thought that the man earns the wrath of his master because he is too conservative with the money entrusted to him. The master entrusted him with one talent, which was a large sum of money, more than fifteen years' wages for a laborer. But he was afraid of losing it, so rather than investing it as did the other two slaves in the story, he took it out and buried it in the yard. Then, when the master wanted his money back, the man returned it and said, "Master, I knew that you were a harsh man, reaping where you did not sow, and gathering where you did not scatter seed, so I was afraid and I went and hid your talent in the ground. Here take what is yours."

As I have been saying, I have always assumed that the man's fault was that he was too conservative with the master's money. But now I am wondering whether I should have been paying attention to something else in the scripture — not just the money itself, but also the man's beliefs about the nature of God, beliefs that filled him with fear. Remember, a parable often invites us to view the world allegorically — things in the parable including people stand for something else. If the master in this parable somehow represents God, then the one-talent man has a rather unflattering image of

God. He said: "Master, I knew that you were a harsh man, reaping where you did not sow, and gathering where you did not scatter seed, so I was afraid and I went and hid your talent in the ground. Here take what is yours."

How did the one-talent guy come to such conclusions? Maybe he had a neighbor or a Sunday school teacher who tried to scare the hell out of him. Maybe he had been reading some bad theology. Maybe he just grew up believing that God is mean, angry, and vindictive.

Ironically, up to this point there is nothing in the parable that would lead to such a conclusion. Quite the opposite, in fact, this master was a generous and caring fellow who entrusted his slaves with large sums of money. He wanted them to succeed, not fail; he wanted them to thrive, not tremble in fear of his wrath. Clearly, the image that the one-talent man had of his master was inconsistent with the picture of the master that Jesus paints for us.

It seems, therefore, that this man is paralyzed, not so much by fiscal conservatism, but by an ill-begotten and fearful belief that the master, that is to say God, is harsh and angry. Is this the God that we want to proclaim? Is this the gospel we want to preach — the angry old man in the nursing home who kicks over the jigsaw puzzles we make of our lives? I hope not!

In a few minutes we will sing one of the grand old hymns of our faith. It contains one of the great phrases in all of Christian hymnody. Referring to God, the hymn proclaims:

> *Thou hast the true and perfect gentleness,*
> *No harshness hast thou and no bitterness:*
> *O grant to us the grace we find in thee,*
> *That we may dwell in perfect unity.*
> ("I Greet Thee, My Sure Redeemer Art," in *The Presbyterian Hymnal* [Louisville: Westminster/John Knox Press, 1990], Hymn 457)

Our hymnal attributes those words to John Calvin, the

French lawyer and pioneer of the Protestant Reformation in sixteenth-century Europe. Whether Calvin actually wrote the hymn is open to some debate. But no one debates that Calvin was the genius behind the Reformed branch of theology, which forms the basis for many of our Presbyterian beliefs, particularly our belief in God's grace.

Ironically, some modern-day historians suggest that Calvin did not always practice what he preached. They accuse him of failing to live according to the gracious and gentle standards, which the hymn attributes to God. The controversy surrounds the life and death of a Spanish physician and theologian by the name of Michael Servetus.

To make a long story short, Servetus thought of himself as a Protestant, but he rejected the traditional Christian belief in the Trinity, that is that God exists as three persons, Father, Son, and Holy Spirit. Because Servetus held this belief, both Catholics and Protestants accused him of heresy, forcing him to flee for his life. Sometime later when Servetus was passing through Geneva, Switzerland, he decided to attend a worship service where John Calvin was the preacher. Someone in the congregation recognized Servetus and after the worship service they arrested him and threw him in prison. Eventually the Protestant Council of Geneva put him on trial and condemned him to death as a heretic. They burned him at the stake.

Some historians blame Calvin for the death of Servetus. They claim that since Calvin held tremendous political and theological power in Geneva, he had the power to stop the execution but did not. However, other historians suggest that Calvin did not desire the death of Servetus, at least not at first. Rather, Calvin wanted him to renounce his heresy. To this end, Calvin visited Servetus in prison, before and after the trial, trying to persuade him to change his beliefs. Additionally, the Protestant Council of Geneva wrote letters to the Protestant leaders of other cities seeking their advice. All wrote back urging the Geneva Council to condemn Servetus to death.

History at this point remains a bit cloudy. Was John Calvin a bloodthirsty reformer who eagerly sought the death of Servetus? Or was he more a reluctant reformer who agreed to the death penalty only after failing to persuade Servetus to change? No one may ever know for sure. However, this is crystal clear — Calvin was as much a product of the violent times in which he lived as anyone else. And today, we might wish that the Council of Geneva had come up with a more gracious and humane punishment for heresy. But that would be like trying to rewrite history.

Whether or not Calvin ever actually wrote the hymn, and whether or not he was a blood-thirsty reformer who eagerly sought the death of Servetus, we may never know. But this we do know. The words of the hymn attributed to him lift before us a gracious view of God that should guide and govern our beliefs, especially when we are tempted to forget them:

> *Thou hast the true and perfect gentleness,*
> *No harshness hast thou and no bitterness:*
> *O grant to us the grace we find in thee,*
> *That we may dwell in perfect unity.*
> ("I Greet Thee, My Sure Redeemer Art," in *The Presbyterian Hymnal* [Louisville: Westminster/John Knox Press, 1990], Hymn 457)

This is the kind of God we should believe in. This is the gospel we should preach.

Amen.

---

1. Tennessee Williams, *The Night of the Iguana* (New York: Penguin Group Publishers, 1976), p. 60.
2. William Barclay, *William Barclay: A Spiritual Autobiography* (Grand Rapids: William B. Eerdmans Publishing Company, 1977), p. 52.
3. Thomas W. Gillespie, "Brother Jesus" in *The Power to Make Things New*, Bruce Larson, ed. (Waco, Texas: Word Books, 1986), pp. 149-150.

Christ the King (Proper 29) /
Pentecost 25 / Ordinary Time 34
Matthew 25:31-46

The Judge of the Living and the Dead

When the Son of Man comes in his glory...he will sit on the throne of his glory...and separate people one from another as a shepherd separates the sheep from the goats.
— Matthew 25:31-32

In a recent essay, Princeton Seminary president Craig Barnes wrote about two black Labrador retrievers that attended worship in the seminary chapel. It's not that these dogs were especially religious. Rather, they were guide dogs trained to help visually impaired students make their way across campus. Barnes noted that when these dogs came to chapel they laid under the front pew and he added, "They always faced the pulpit."

> *It's a fascinating experience to look down from the pulpit, halfway through the sermon's best sentence that was oh so carefully prepared, and see a couple of tired dogs looking up at me.*[1]

Barnes used the pulpit and the dogs to illustrate the main point of his essay. He said:

> *I am struck by how many preachers keep finding ways to give the bad-dog sermon, in both conservative and progressive congregations. The pastor stands in the pulpit and scolds the world for being a mess, then scolds the congregation for allowing this mess to continue.*[2]

In light of Barnes' essay, I have been pondering my own preaching over the years, and have to admit that I too have preached some "Bad Dog!" sermons. I had a good friend in our Chicago congregation who always accused me of preaching what he called "angry" sermons in the fall of the year. I said to him, "That's because it's stewardship season and I grow impatient with people who drive fancy cars and live in beautiful homes and yet pledge just a pittance to Christ and the church." He countered by saying, "I think those angry sermons are because sailing season just ended and you've hauled your boat for the winter!" Perhaps, we were both a little bit right.

In one of his books, popular philosopher, William Fulghum wrote about the German town of Ulm, where in the sixteenth century there lived a man named Hans Babblinger. He was a dreamer and inventor who believed that someday human beings would fly. He created some wings, went to the foothills of the Bavarian Alps where upcurrents of wind are common, and strapped the wings to his back. In the presence of some reliable witnesses, he jumped off a high hill and soared safely downward. Sensational! Babblinger could fly.

Not long after, King Ludwig and his royal court came to town and the local leaders wanted to impress him. "Get Hans Babblinger to fly for the king," they said. Everybody thought it was a grand idea. Unfortunately, the demonstration took place, not in the hills of the Alps with their upcurrents of wind, but on the bluffs of the Danube River where the wind currents blow downward. Babblinger stood on a high platform, waved to the crowd, and jumped into the air only to plunge like a cannon ball into the river. The demonstration was a total flop.

The next Sunday, the Bishop of Ulm stood in the pulpit of the cathedral church, called Babblinger by name during the sermon and chastised him for the sin of pride. "Man was not meant to fly!" thundered the bishop. Humiliated in front of a cathedral full of people, Babblinger left the church that day, made a beeline for his home and never ever appeared in public again. Not long after he died, probably of a broken heart.

One day several hundred years later Robert Fulghum was a passenger on a glider, floating through the air at 5,000 feet! Down near the ground he could see several hot air balloons, an ultralight aircraft, and several other gliders. Up above, a 747 climbed to 40,000 feet on its way to Chicago or New York. As Fulghum floated through the air, he thought about old Hans Babblinger and that day when there came from the pulpit of a Christian church a message against him of judgment and condemnation. Fulghum said this about the pulpit:

> *Historically, the symbol of the pulpit has been the pointing, damning finger, accusing men and women of sin, failure, wickedness, inequities, and the pride of thinking for themselves, telling them that in this life there is no hope, in this life there is no glory. I say the pulpit should stand for wings, not angel wings or eagle wings or any other wings you've ever seen, but wings of the Holy Spirit that lift hearts and minds to high places.*[3]

As long as I am privileged to serve as your minister, I hope that this pulpit will always stand for that — not a pointing, damning finger, but the wings of the Holy Spirit that lift hearts and minds to high places.

And yet… having just said all of that, I still feel the need to speak, at least occasionally, about the judgment of God. Judgment is not a minor theme in the Bible, after all, but a major one.
- What is the expulsion of Adam and Eve from the Garden of Eden after they ate the forbidden fruit other than an example of God's judgment?
- What is the story of the golden calf other than an illustration of worshiping the wrong God?

- What is the purpose of the prophets of Israel other than to say that God is displeased because the people like sheep have wandered astray?

In the New Testament we also find a fair measure of God's judgment. In the gospel of Luke, for example, Jesus told a story about a rich fool, a wealthy farmer who had a particularly successful harvest. "What should I do?" he said to himself, "for I have no place to store my crops?" Then he said, "I know what I'll do. I'll pull down my barns and build larger ones and there I will store all my grain. And I'll say to myself, 'Self, you've done very well. You've made enough to retire early. Go out and buy the biggest mobile home you can and take off and see the country. Get one of those bumper stickers that boasts, "We're spending our grandchildren's inheritance." Have the time of your life. Eat, drink, be merry.' "

But God said to him, "You fool! This very night, your life is being demanded of you." And the mobile home? What good will that be when they close the lid of your casket and lower you into the ground? (See Luke 12:18-20.) You can almost taste God's judgment when the rich fool comes face to face with his own selfish choices.

Not long after, Jesus told another story about God's judgment, the story about the rich man who dressed in Brooks Brothers' Suits and feasted on champagne and surf and turf. Meanwhile, just beyond the rich man's gated community, just outside the range of his security alarm, there laid a poor man who was starving to death. He would gladly have fed himself on the scraps of food the rich man scraped down the garbage disposal. Time went by and both men died. The poor man went to heaven, while the rich man ended up in hell, where he pleaded with Abraham for another chance. But Abraham replied, "Child, remember that during your lifetime you received your good things, and Lazarus in like manner evil things; but now he is comforted here in heaven and you are in agony" (Luke 16:19-31). You get the sense that Jesus had judged the rich man and found him lacking because he failed to show compassion toward the poor man.

Of all the Bible's words about judgment, there are none more striking than those from this morning's second lesson: the parable of Jesus often called the Great Judgment, or the Final Judgment. More than likely, it's what the writers' of the Apostles' Creed had in mind with the words that Jesus will come to judge the quick (by which we mean the living) and the dead. Speaking of himself as the Son of Man, Jesus said that he would sit on his throne and judge all the nations of the world, separating the people into two groups as a shepherd separates the sheep from the goats. According to the parable, the blessed are those who feed the hungry, welcome the strangers, clothe the naked, minister to the sick, and visit those in prison. On the other hand, those who do not perform these gracious acts of kindness and mercy get dragged away to eternal punishment (Matthew 25:31-46). Referring to this parable Mother Teresa once said, "At the end of life, we will not be judged by diplomas, money, or the great things we have done. We will be judged by, 'I was hungry and you gave me something to eat, I was naked and you clothed me, I was homeless and you took me in.' "

And so on this the final Sunday of the church year — Christ the King Sunday — we are left with this unsettling message about God's judgment. It is a message that most of us would rather not hear. It is a message that, frankly, I would rather not preach. In the face of such a message, some of us might sink into hopelessness and despair. But I believe that others will hear in these words not hopelessness, but a glorious challenge to live lives of service and self-sacrifice. Of course, the bottom line is still this: No matter how good we think we have been, when the time comes and we stand before Jesus, the righteous judge, seated at the right hand of God, each of us will want to hope and pray that the judge will be merciful.

Amen.

1. M. Craig Barnes, "Good Dog, Bad Dog" in *The Christian Century*, November 12, 2014, p. 35.
2. *Ibid.*
3. Robert Fulghum, *It Was on Fire When I Lay Down on It* (New York: Ivy Books, 1988), pp. 183-185.

Thanksgiving Day
Luke 17:11-19

Choosing to Be Grateful

Then Jesus asked, "Were not ten made clean? But the other nine, where are they?"
— Luke 17:17

There was once a minister who was well known for his beautiful and moving prayers. He always knew just what to say because, I am told, his heart overflowed with gratitude. But one Sunday morning he woke up to the kind of day we preachers dread. If it was not a full-blown nor'easter, it came pretty close. The wind was howling and the rain was coming down in sheets. As a result, many people stayed home from worship, while those who braved the elements and came to church wondered what the minister would say. Typically, he filled his prayers with praise and thanksgiving. But how could he be thankful on such a miserable day? Indeed, as he stood up to pray, the ushers at the back of the church were even placing small bets that he couldn't pull it off. But the minister did not disappoint for with utter honesty he prayed, "O God, we thank you... that it is not always as bad as this."

Recently, I had a chance to test that minister's philosophy for myself when my wife and I went off for a week's vacation on *Morning Star*, our family's sailboat. Although Monday dawned with beautiful weather and a warm southerly breeze that pushed us some forty miles up the Chesapeake Bay, by Tuesday the weather started to deteriorate and the weather forecasters started using that dreaded word — Nor'easter. Tuesday morning we motored into a safe and well-protected creek behind Gwynn's Island, set both of our anchors, and prepared to stay put until the storm passed. As predicted, the strong winds and the driving rain arrived late Tuesday. But then Tuesday became Wednesday… and Wednesday became Thursday… with no sign that the storm was letting up. I began thinking about Noah, bobbing around in the ark for forty days and forty nights and wondering if we would ever get back home. Then I began thinking about a more immediate concern. After two and a half days of torrential rain, in which my wife and I were confined to the little cabin of our boat, I looked up from the book I was reading, *Ten Great Dates to Energize Your Marriage*, and realizing that this sailing vacation was not one of them, I said nervously, "Betsy, do you still love me?"

By Friday, the rain was still falling, but the winds began to moderate, so we hauled in our anchors, pointed the bow of the boat down the Bay and arrived back home seven damp and dreary hours later. As we slogged our way South that Friday and on several days since, I've had plenty of time to ponder our trip. It was by far the worst sailing vacation I've ever been on. But like the minister who prayed, "God, we thank you that it is not always as bad as this," I surprised no one more than myself when I still found reasons to be grateful:

- I was grateful for a well-protected creek with tall trees and our two strong anchors with which we rode out the storm;
- Grateful for a seaworthy boat, which got us safely up and down the Bay;
- Grateful for smart phones that kept us up to date with the latest weather and allowed us to stay in touch with our kids;
- Grateful for good food and wine, which warmed our hearts and gladdened our spirits even when we were wet and cold;
- Grateful for the bald eagle we spotted one afternoon, soaring majestically above the trees and then feasting on a large fish that had washed up on the shore;

- Grateful for books to read and backgammon and scrabble to help us pass the time.
- And most of all, I was grateful that when I asked "Do you still love me?" Betsy replied with a resounding, "Yes!"

As I've thought about the trip, a single idea has been running through my mind. Gratitude is something you choose. It begins when you become aware of the gifts of God's that are all around you, if only you will open your eyes to perceive them. How easy it would have been to complain about the rain, the wind, and the storm, which at one level turned our week's vacation into a bust! Instead, I felt God was nudging me to open my eyes and my heart to the blessings of a bald eagle, the smell of savory food, a loving spouse, and a safe and secure anchorage. Gratitude is something you choose.

Karl Barth, the great twentieth-century theologian, went even farther. He claimed that gratitude is a major part of living a Christian life. Someone once asked him, "How do you know that you are a Christian?" Do you know how he answered? He said, "Because I am grateful." Now that is not to say that we Christians have cornered the market on gratitude. Jews, Muslims, Buddhists and even people of no faith at all can also live lives of gratitude. But it is to say that one of the marks of being a Christian is our gratitude. In fact, to call yourself a Christian and then live an ungrateful life is a contradiction of terms. Craig Barnes, who is now the president of Princeton Seminary, once wrote, "Gratitude may be the ultimate vocation for the Christian."[1] God may call you to do any number of things with your life:
- to accept a job in a new city,
- to teach a Sunday school class,
- to sing in the choir, or volunteer at the shelter,
- to go off on a mission trip,
- to arrange flowers for Sunday worship,
- to work to make a difference in someone's life.

God may be calling you to do any number of things, but ultimately God is calling you to respond to the blessings of life by living a life of gratitude.

But here's the challenge. Although gratitude is something we choose, it does not come naturally — not for you and not for me. Church historian Martin Marty once called gratitude a "learned behavior," which is why we need to teach little children to say "thank you." In fact, adds Marty, "The President of the United States even needs to *proclaim* Thanksgiving Day to an otherwise distracted and pre-occupied nation."[2]

Maybe the one leper in Jesus' parable returned to give thanks simply because his parents raised him to do so. But most people are brought up to say "thank you," even, I imagine, the other nine lepers in Jesus' parable. Why, then, did they fail to say "thank you" in this instance? No one knows for sure, but maybe it's because they felt entitled to their healing. Maybe they felt like they deserved it. Certainly, there was a part of me that felt entitled to a week of nice weather for my vacation. "I work hard," I might have said to myself. "I even try to do the Lord's work. The least God could do would be to send some blue skies and gentle winds in my direction!"

But life doesn't work like that — not for me, not for you and not for those ten lepers. When blessings come our way they come as free and unmerited gifts, not because we earned them or deserve them or are entitled to them. Perhaps the Samaritan leper understood this better than the others, since as a religious "outsider" he was not used to all of life's advantages.

As I thought back to our sailing trip, I began to sense a couple of things that helped me to be grateful. One of them was Psalm 65, which along with the story of the ten lepers is also one the recommended lessons for Thanksgiving Day. Isn't it amazing the way that God speaks to us through the scriptures, calling us out of our own little world and inviting us to behold the beauty and wonder of God's world? Here I was sitting in the little cabin of our boat, socked in because of the weather, feeling sorry for myself when I decided to read ahead in the lectionary. When I came to the words of Psalm 65, a psalm of thanksgiving for earth's bounty, it was as if the Spirit was urging me to be grateful:

- Grateful that God answers prayer.
- Grateful that God forgives our transgressions.
- Grateful for the goodness of God's holy house, this church and all other places of worship.
- Grateful for the gift of salvation.
- Grateful that God silences the roaring sea. (Well, maybe not as quickly as my wife and I were hoping!)
- Grateful for the way that God "softens the earth with showers and blesses its growth."
- Grateful that God crowns the year with bounty.

In addition to Psalm 65, the other thing that prompted my gratitude was a book I read while we were away. As you may know, I read a lot of books but rarely does a book move me the way this one did. It's called, *Love and Death: My Journey Through the Valley of the Shadow*, and it was written by a Unitarian minister by the name of Forrest Church, who was diagnosed with terminal cancer of the esophagus at age 58. Sadly, this turned out to be his final book. He died from that cancer just three years later.

With incredible bravery, he described his battle with cancer as well as his final three years, and weaves throughout the book his own philosophy of life.

- "Religion," he wrote, "is our human response to the dual reality of being alive and having to die."[3]
- "Death," he wrote, "is not life's goal, only life's terminus. The goal of life is to live in such a way that our lives will prove worth dying for. This is where love comes into the picture. The one thing that can't be taken from us, even by death, is the love we give away before we die."[4]

- "Life is not a given," he added. "Life is a wondrous gift. That gift comes with a price attached. One day something will steal it from us. That doesn't diminish our lives; it increases their value. Earlier in my life," he wrote, "it took a crazed driver in a car which almost ran over my children and me to awaken me once again to the wonder of life and the blessings of love."[5]

As I sat in the cabin of our boat and pondered the brave and beautiful, life-in-the-face-of-death words such as these, my own problems seemed silly by comparison. So rather than complaining about a vacation that didn't turn out the way that I had hoped, instead, I felt compelled to open my eyes to the beauty and wonders of God's goodness. I chose to be grateful. And, frankly, that makes a world of difference in anyone's approach to life. As one of our great old hymns puts it:

All good gifts around us
are sent from heaven above,
Then thank the Lord,
O thank the Lord,
For all of his love.
("We Plow the Fields and Scatter," in *The Presbyterian Hymnal* [Louisville: Westminster/John Knox Press, 1990], Hymn 560)

Amen.

---

1. M. Craig Barnes, *When God Interrupts* (Downers Grove: InterVarsity Press, 1996), p. 95.
2. Martin Marty and Micah Marty, *Our Hope for Years to Come* (Minneapolis: Augsburg Fortress, 1995), p. 100.
3. Forrest Church, *Love and Death: My Journey Through the Valley of the Shadow* (Boston: Beacon Press, 2008), p. x.
4. *Ibid.*
5. *Ibid.*, p. 43.

Another CSS Title by Albert G. Butzer, III

Tears of Sadness, Tears of Gladness
Gospel Sermons for Lent/Easter, Cycle A
Albert G. Butzer, III
0-7880-1823-X
5.5 x 8.5
116 pages

www.ingramcontent.com/pod-product-compliance
Lightning Source LLC
Chambersburg PA
CBHW071750040426
42446CB00012B/2513